W9-AJS-942

EDGE
BOOKS™

SUPER TRIVIA COLLECTION

THIS BOOK'S GOT GAME

BY HANS HETRICK

A COLLECTION OF AWESOME SPORTS TRIVIA

CAPSTONE PRESS
a capstone imprint

Edge Books are published by Capstone Press,
1710 Roe Crest Drive, North Mankato, Minnesota 56003.
www.capstonepub.com

 Books published by Capstone Press are manufactured with paper
containing at least 10 percent post-consumer waste.

Library of Congress Cataloging-in-Publication Data
Hetrick, Hans, 1973–
   This book's got game : a collection of awesome sports trivia / by Hans Hetrick.
      p. cm. — (Super trivia collection)
   Includes bibliographical references and index.
   Summary: "Describes a variety of trivia facts about sports"—Provided by publisher.
   ISBN 978-1-4296-7656-4 (hardcover)
   1. Sports—Miscellanea—Juvenile literature. I. Title. II. Series.
   GV707.H48 2012
   796—dc23   2011035743

Editorial Credits
Angie Kaelberer, editor; Alison Thiele, designer; Svetlana Zhurkin, media researcher;
   Laura Manthe, production specialist

Photo Credits
AP Photo, 12 (top), Chris O'Meara, 13 (top), Nikitin, cover (bottom right), 6 (top), Reed
Saxon, cover (bottom left), 8 (top); Corbis: Bettmann, 8 (bottom), 10 (bottom), 13 (bottom),
14, 21 (top), 27 (top); Dreamstime: Michael Flippo, 18 (bottom), Yobro10, 15 (bottom right);
Library of Congress, 7 (all), 9 (bottom), 11 (all), 16 (top); Newscom: Icon SMI, 19, Icon
SMI/Allen Fredrickson, 20 (middle), Icon SMI/Brian Pohorylo, 15 (top), Icon SMI/Diane
Moore, 25 (top), Icon SMI/John McDonough, 26 (top), Icon SMI/Shawn Jordan, 10 (top),
Icon SMI/Tony Donaldson, 9 (top), RTR/Suzanne Plunkett, 23 (top), Sipa/Photocome, 24
(right), SportsChrome/Tom DiPace, 27 (bottom); Shutterstock: Clipart deSIGN, 12 (bottom),
Danomyte, 22 (bottom), Domenic Gareri, 17 (top), ehammer, 22 (top right), ekler, 17
(bottom), elm, 23 (bottom), Eray Arpaci, 3 (bottom), 6 (bottom), Fejas, 22 (top left), Fernando Cortes
(background), throughout, Harper, 16 (bottom), iofoto, 21 (bottom), irin-k (soccer ball),
cover, 1, Ken Durden, 18 (top), Mikhail Popov, 28, Nick Stubbs, 29, Pete Niesen, 4–5, Sapik,
1 (bottom), 26 (bottom), Steve Cukrov, 24 (left), Takeiteasy Art, 20 (top), titelio, 15 (bottom
left), Trinacria Photo (football), cover, 1, Ventura, 25 (bottom), Walter G. Arce, 22 (middle)

Printed in the United States of America in Stevens Point, Wisconsin.
072012   006856R

TABLE OF CONTENTS

INCREDIBLE SPORTS

Can you imagine the world without sports? It's not a pretty thought. A world with no skateboards, no Super Bowl, and no Olympics would be a sad place.

Sports have been around almost as long as people have lived on Earth. Ancient people threw, kicked, and caught balls. They wrestled each other. They raced. And they developed rules about how their sports should be played. Sports give us plenty of reasons to play. This book is a collection of everything that's fun about the world of sports!

FEOFANOVA
RUS   2778
ATT.1 4.55

Chapter 1
AMAZING ATHLETES

The greatest athletes never stop pushing the limits. That winning spirit was clear in the tiny gymnast who showed the world perfection. It was there in the baseball player who took the field for every game during 16 seasons. These athletes and others have expanded the limits of what's possible.

During his 27-year career, Major League Baseball (MLB) pitcher Nolan Ryan made failure a family affair when he struck out eight fathers and their sons. They were Bobby and Barry Bonds; Ken and Ken Griffey Jr.; Maury and Bump Wills; Sandy, Sandy Jr., and Roberto Alomar; Hal and Brian McRae; Dick and Dick Jr. Schofield; Tony and Eduardo Perez; and Tito and Terry Francona.

Former National Basketball Association (NBA) player Shaquille O'Neal's shoe size is 22. The average shoe size for men is 10.5!

Sports fans were amazed when Bo Jackson and Deion Sanders played both pro baseball and football. For Jim Thorpe, two sports was a slow year! In the 1912 Olympics, Thorpe won gold medals in the **decathlon** and the **pentathlon**. Thorpe was a pro football star from 1913 until 1928. He also played six years of Major League Baseball and toured with a pro basketball team.

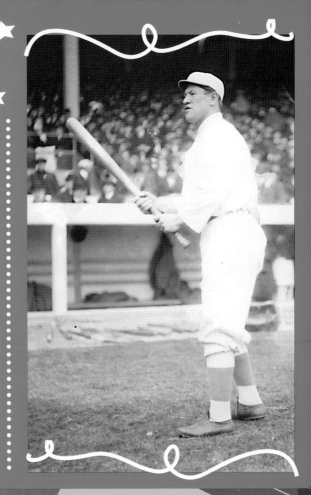

Jackie Robinson was an MLB legend. As a student at UCLA, Robinson became the first athlete to earn a **letter** in four sports. Oddly enough, he was the least successful in baseball!

decathlon—a track-and-field contest made up of 10 events
pentathlon—a track-and-field contest made up of five events
letter—an award, usually a patch in the shape of a letter, given to athletes who play a high school or college sport

You don't earn a nickname like "The Great One" without breaking a few records. Wayne Gretzky holds or shares 61 National Hockey League (NHL) records. His 2,857 career points are almost 1,000 points more than any other hockey player. Gretzky is the only NHL player to total more than 200 points in a single season. And he did it four times!

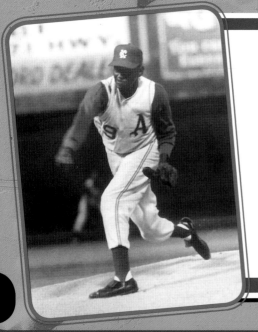

The great Satchel Paige is the oldest player to appear in an MLB game. In 1965, 59-year-old Paige pitched for the Kansas City A's. He shut down the Boston Red Sox for three innings.

Even great athletes have to practice. Tony Hawk spent 10 years trying to nail skateboarding's most difficult trick, the 900. At the 1999 X Games, Hawk dropped off the half-pipe and spun around 2½ times in the air. He had landed the first 900!

Wilt "The Stilt" Chamberlain was an NBA record-setting machine. Chamberlain, who played from 1959 to 1974, still holds 72 NBA records. His most famous record is his 100-point game against the New York Knicks in 1962. During his career, Chamberlain never fouled out of a game. And during the 1961–62 NBA season, Chamberlain played almost every minute of every game. Except for a six-minute stretch in one game, he stayed on the court from the tip-off to the final buzzer.

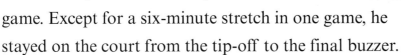

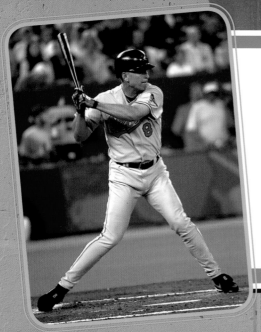

For 2,632 consecutive games, Cal Ripken Jr. took the field for the Baltimore Orioles. Ripken never missed an Orioles game from May 1982 to September 1998.

Tom Dempsey was born with the fingers missing from his right hand and the toes missing from his right foot. That didn't stop him from setting a record for the longest field goal in National Football League (NFL) history. Dempsey kicked a 63-yard (58-meter) field goal for the New Orleans Saints in 1970.

Reggie Jackson, Albert Pujols, and Babe Ruth are the only players to hit three home runs in a single World Series game. In Game 6 of the 1977 World Series, Jackson hit his three home runs on the first pitch of his last three at bats—three pitches, three swings, and three home runs.

Babe Ruth ★

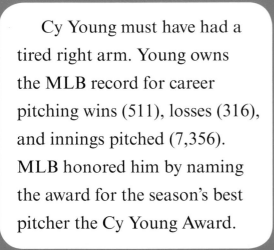

Cy Young must have had a tired right arm. Young owns the MLB record for career pitching wins (511), losses (316), and innings pitched (7,356). MLB honored him by naming the award for the season's best pitcher the Cy Young Award.

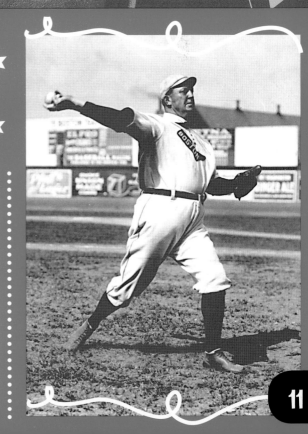

Fourteen-year-old Nadia Comaneci charmed the entire world at the 1976 Montreal Olympics. The girl from Romania became the first gymnast to score a perfect 10. She finished with seven perfect 10s and three gold medals!

Who says football is only for guys? In 1997 kicker Liz Heaston became the first female player to score in a college football game. Heaston kicked two extra points to help win a game for Oregon's Willamette University.

On September 23, 1992, Manon Rheaume became the first woman to play in one of the four major U.S. pro sports leagues. She played goalie for the Tampa Bay Lightning in a pre-season game.

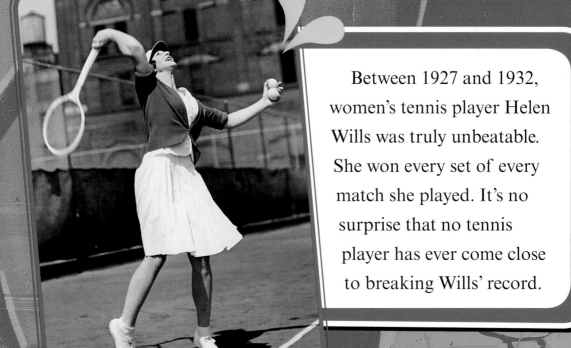

Between 1927 and 1932, women's tennis player Helen Wills was truly unbeatable. She won every set of every match she played. It's no surprise that no tennis player has ever come close to breaking Wills' record.

Chapter 2
TREMENDOUS TEAMS

When teams work together and play well, they inspire their fans. With thousands of fans behind them, teams can achieve more than they could by themselves.

The 1972 Miami Dolphins are the only NFL team to finish an entire season with a perfect record. Since then, no NFL team has survived a season without at least one loss.

There is only one U.S. city where each major sports team wears the same colors. The Pittsburgh Penguins, Steelers, and Pirates all wear black and gold.

In 2008 the University of Connecticut women's basketball team started an amazing winning streak. When the Lady Huskies finally lost in 2010, they had won 90 straight games and two National Collegiate Athletic Association (NCAA) titles.

The 1916 Georgia Tech football team scored more points in one game than any two teams combined. The Yellow Jackets crushed Cumberland College of Tennessee, 222-0. This score still stands as a record for most points by one football team and most points scored in one football game.

Years ago, so many trolleys sped down the streets of Brooklyn, New York, that people there were called "trolley-dodgers." When it came time to name their baseball team, the Dodgers made perfect sense. Now that the team is in Los Angeles, the meaning is lost.

Only nine major sports teams in the United States and Canada have a nickname that doesn't end with an "s."

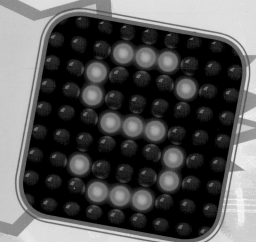

trolley—an electric street car that runs on tracks

What's with the name?

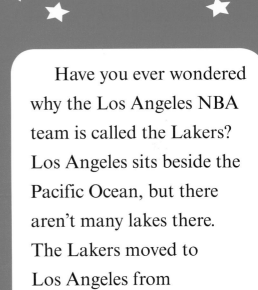

Have you ever wondered why the Los Angeles NBA team is called the Lakers? Los Angeles sits beside the Pacific Ocean, but there aren't many lakes there. The Lakers moved to Los Angeles from Minnesota, known as the land of 10,000 lakes.

NFL helmets were just plain boring until 1948. That year, the Los Angeles Rams painted yellow horns on their helmets. Today the Cleveland Browns are the only team without a helmet logo.

Chapter 3
UNEXPECTED EVENTS

Sports events don't have a script. There is always a chance that something unexpected could happen.

Today a Super Bowl ticket can cost more than $1,000. But the tickets weren't always so valued. At Super Bowl I in 1967, the Los Angeles Memorial Coliseum had more than 30,000 empty seats. Some tickets sold for as little as $6!

In a 1993 AFC playoff game, the Buffalo Bills trailed the Houston Oilers 35-3 in the second half. Many Bills fans figured their team had no chance to win and left. These fans were sorry later when the Bills scored four touchdowns to win 41-38 in overtime.

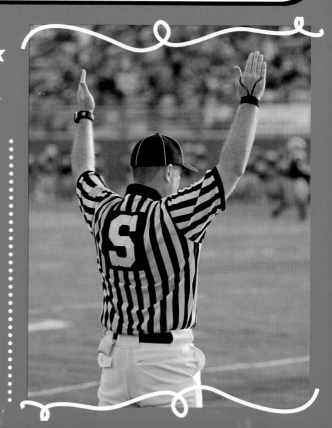

On December 31, 1967, the Green Bay Packers and Dallas Cowboys faced off in the legendary Ice Bowl. It was the NFL title game. The winner wasn't decided until the last second. But it was the cold that made the game memorable. The temperature in Green Bay, Wisconsin, at game time was -13 degrees Fahrenheit (-25° Celsius). Nearly two dozen fans went to the hospital suffering from exposure, and four had heart attacks. Tragically, one died.

Unusual Adventures

OUTRAGEOUS
AWESOME SPORTS
TRIVIA

Each member of the NHL championship team gets to spend a day with the event trophy, the Stanley Cup. Over the years, the cup has been part of some unusual adventures. Martin Brodeur of the 2003 New Jersey Devils ate popcorn out of it at a movie theater. In 1906 the Montreal Wanderers took the cup to a photographer's house for a team photo. The team left the house without the cup. The photographer's mother found it and planted flowers in it. In 1980 the New York Islanders' Clark Gillies let his dog eat out of the cup. Since 1995 the cup has had a 24-hour bodyguard. Players can still have fun with the cup, but the bodyguard is always there to protect it.

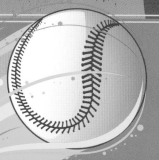

There are only two days during the year in which there is no MLB, NBA, NHL, or NFL game. They occur the day before and the day after the MLB All-Star game.

Stretching is good!

The seventh-inning stretch is part of all MLB games. It's believed to have started at Manhattan College in 1882. During a game, baseball coach Brother Jasper Brennan saw that the crowd was restless. In the seventh inning, he turned and urged the fans to stand up and stretch. The stretch caught on and soon spread to the major leagues.

Only one pitcher has thrown a **perfect game** in the World Series. New York Yankee Don Larsen pitched a perfect game in Game 5 of the 1956 World Series.

Since the World Series began in 1903, it has been held during two world wars and an earthquake. But there were two years it didn't happen. In 1904 the New York Giants of the National League refused to play the American League champs, the Boston Americans. In 1994 MLB players went on **strike**, and the World Series had to be canceled.

Where are all the fans?

perfect game—a game in which a pitcher doesn't allow a single batter to reach first base and there are no hits or runs
strike—to refuse to work until demands are met

During a NASCAR race, the temperature inside the cars climbs as high as 140°F (60°C). Drivers can lose 5 to 10 pounds (2.3 to 4.5 kg) during a race.

10

At 200 miles (322 kilometers) per hour, a NASCAR car can travel 293 feet (89 m) in one second. That's nearly the length of a football field!

During turns NASCAR drivers can experience 3 units of g-force against their bodies. This is the same amount of force that astronauts on a space shuttle experience at liftoff!

Nicolas Mahut ★

How much longer?

John Isner ★

Wimbledon is the world's most famous tennis tournament. In 2010 it was the site of the longest professional tennis match—11 hours and 5 minutes. John Isner and Nicolas Mahut began playing the evening of June 22 before darkness fell. The game resumed June 23 before again being called for darkness. After an hour of play on June 24, Isner finally won the match.

Is a race still a race with only one competitor? Triple Crown winner Citation entered the 1948 Pimlico Special along with 20 other racehorses. When the other owners saw Citation was running, they got scared and pulled their horses out of the race. Citation ran the race alone.

Chapter 4

STRANGE BUT TRUE

Sports are always a little bit out of the ordinary. From a sport founded by a toy maker to boxers knocking each other out at the same time, sports supply a lot of strange surprises.

In 2005 skateboarder Danny Way decided to jump over the Great Wall of China. The wall is 61 feet (19 m) wide. Way designed a ramp to help him jump over the wall. He cleared the wall five times, even doing tricks during some of the jumps.

Piece of cake!

Most kids use a baseball until it falls apart. But a baseball used in MLB games has an average life span of only six pitches. With between 250 and 300 pitches per game, that's 49 to 50 balls that don't make it to the next game!

Freestyle motocross star Travis Pastrana had an extreme dream. In 2001 he made it come true. He used a parachute to jump his motorcycle into the Grand Canyon. He free-fell 1,000 feet (305 m) and then pulled the parachute, which allowed him to float the last 500 feet (152 m) to the canyon floor.

Can you believe a major sport started with a toy? In 1965 Sherman Popper invented a toy called a Snurfer, which was short for "snow surfer." It was basically two skis tied together, with a rope at the front for steering. Popper's invention led to the snowboards of today.

Shortstop Zoilo Versalles threw away his baseball glove after every **error**. During Versalles' 12-year MLB career, he made 284 errors. That's a lot of baseball gloves! But pitcher Jim Kaat found a glove he really liked—he used the same one for 15 seasons!

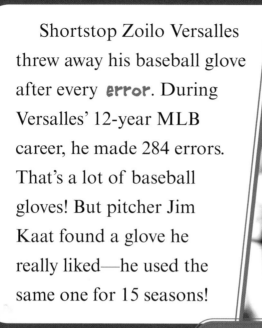

Jim Kaat ★

In 1940 Montreal Royals' third baseman Bert Haas hurried up to field a bunt. When Haas realized he couldn't throw the batter out, he got down on his knees. He took a deep breath and blew the ball into foul territory. The umpire ruled the ball foul!

error—a fielder's misplay that allows a batter to reach one or more bases

The sport of stock car racing traces its roots to **bootleggers** of the 1920s. To get away from the police, bootleggers modified their cars to handle high speeds and sharp turns. Soon the bootleggers began racing each other. The races started to attract crowds, and stock car racing was born.

If you want your team to win the Super Bowl, make sure your quarterback wears number 12! A quarterback wearing that number has played for the winning team in 1969, 1972–80, 2002, 2004–05, and 2011.

bootlegger—a person who sells illegally made alcohol

During a 1912 lightweight title fight, boxers Ad Wolgast and Joe Rivers knocked each other out at the same time. The referee favored Wolgast. He picked him up off the mat and declared him the winner.

Unusual Nicknames

Popular athletes often have unusual nicknames. William "The Refrigerator" Perry was 6 feet, 2 inches (188 centimeters) and 325 pounds (147 kilograms) when he played for the Chicago Bears. Fans thought he looked like a refrigerator. Race car driver A.J. "Fancy Pants" Foyt earned his nickname by showing up for races in silk shirts and white pants. And Larry "Lawnmower" Csonka was a tough running back for the Miami Dolphins in the 1970s. He didn't pick up his feet when he ran, so teammates said he looked like a lawnmower.

WORLD OF SPORTS

The world of sports can be crazy, amazing, and just plain wacky, but most of all, it's fun. Whether you're an athlete or a fan, there's much to love about the wild, wonderful world of sports!

GLOSSARY

bootlegger (BOOT-leger)—a person who sells illegally made alcohol

decathlon (di-KATH-lon)—a track-and-field contest made up of 10 events

error (ER-ur)—a misplay of a ball when normal play would have resulted in an out or prevented an advance by the opposing team

letter (LET-ur)—an award, usually a patch in the shape of a letter, given to athletes who play a high school or college sport

pentathlon (pen-TATH-lon)—a track-and-field contest made up of five events

perfect game (PUR-fikt GAME)—a game in which a pitcher doesn't allow a single batter to reach first base and there are no hits or runs

strike (STRIKE)—to refuse to work until a set of demands is met

trolley (TROL-ee)—an electric street car that runs on tracks and gets power from an overhead wire

umpire (UHM-pire)—an official who rules on plays in baseball, tennis, and other sports

READ MORE

Gilpin, Daniel. *Record-Breaking People.* Record Breakers. New York: PowerKids Press, 2012.

Sports Illustrated for Kids, ed. *Sports Illustrated Kids All Access: Your Behind-the-Scences Pass to Sports Stars, Locker Rooms, and More.* Sports Illustrated Kids. New York: Time Books, 2010.

Raatma, Lucia. *The Curious, Captivating, Unusual History of Sports.* Unusual Histories. Mankato, Minn.: Capstone Press, 2012.

INTERNET SITES

FactHound offers a safe, fun way to find Internet sites related to this book. All of the sites on FactHound have been researched by our staff.

Here's all you do:

Visit *www.facthound.com*

Type in this code: 9781429676564

Check out projects, games and lots more at
www.capstonekids.com

INDEX